SOS:
Staffing's on Steroids

SOS:
Staffing's on Steroids

YOUR PERSONAL GUIDE TO THE WORLD OF PUBLIC AND SPECIAL EDUCATION

P.L. Frederick

Ordering Information:

For orders and inquiries, please contact:
1-888-404-1388
www.goldtouchpress.com
book.orders@goldtouchpress.com

Printed in the United States of America

CONTENTS

"When resources are scarce and a teacher's time is limited, the easiest solution to the problem child may be drug therapy or transfer to a different class. Neither route may be necessary to change or control a child's behavior. However, in some cases, individual attention or skill training may achieve the same end without unnecessary trauma to the child. In the educational environment, "quality-first teaching" is an example of a step in this direction. Recognizing educators need support in the classroom environment in order to fully implement the intent of The Individuals with Disabilities Act, (IDEA, Part H of P.L.101-476) of 1990. This approach represents an attempt by schools to help teachers make adjustments in their instructional methods first rather than referring children for assessment and diagnosis or removing children from this classroom for services."

(Dimensions of Human Behavior, The Changing Life Course, Second Edition pg.237; Elizabeth D. Hutchinson)

This book is dedicated with much love to the
Treasures of our nation: the children.

INTRODUCTION

"My God is within me and He knows what I Need." I breathed as I turned off the ignition to my car. I wiped the tear slipping down my cheek, pulled my purse onto my shoulder and headed into my nine-year-old son's school for a staffing.

The last one was a nightmare. There were six or seven school employees and me. The principal, vice-principal, current teacher, her assistant, social worker, psychiatrist, or psychologist, Along with the director of the area agency for special education and his/her assistant. Don't forget the new teacher. Their collective opinion was my son should be medicated and hospitalized. He had kicked down the door on the "time-out" room an ultimately escaped. They even presented me a bill for one oak door, $35.00.

I refused. My child in no way needed drugged or hospitalized. We had come to an impasse; he could not go to school and I would not drug or hospitalize so the fifth-grade teacher across from my son's, fourth grade room had been coming to our home.

About the third time this teacher came to our house, there was an interesting development. On all three occasions, my son would go to the bathroom forever. The third time, I asked him if there was a problem with this teacher.

I was totally unprepared for what followed. The world stopped and everything seem to unfold in slow motion. I slowly sat on the arm of the couch next to my little boy to clarify what I had just heard, which was in his little nine-year-old voice: "Why is one of the same ones who were helping to lock me in the closet coming to my house?" He proceeded to explain, his teacher, her assistant, the principal, janitor and this teacher would take him by he hands and feet and lock him in the closet. No windows, no light and a hook latch he drew for me. We did not have a lock comparable anywhere in our house.

I sent him upstairs to play as this teacher approached the front door. Inviting him in, directing him to the dining room table, we both sat down. I told him I had a question; looked him in the eye and told him what my son had said. He hung his head and apologized. I stood informing him there was no need for him to return and escorted him out

I called my Pastor who had been counselling all of us due to the mystery involving my son's behaviors. He would totally freak if he thought he was in trouble. We couldn't understand it. He is an only child, both parents in the home, my husband working and although we opted for me to be an at home mom, I was student teaching second grade when he was born.

In preparation for this staffing, my Pastor had given me a written statement to present the "Staffing Team." It said my son's behaviors were a product of his classroom environment. He would acclimate to his surroundings. Being in a behavior disabled had caused him to take on the behaviors of his classmates. Pastor further noted; placing him in a dark padded closet was a completely inappropriate method of discipline for any child. Furthermore, he was available if needed.

In addition, my aunt had been a pediatric charge nurse for forty years, she in no way agreed with the diagnosis.

I am writing this in an effort to assist other parents who find themselves fighting for their child's life.

BE YOUR OWN BEST ADVOCATE

Advocate: "one argues for a cause," or "pleads in another's behalf." (American Heritage Dictionary, pg. 13, 1994. In order to be effective as an advocate, one would have to be knowledgeable of the issues involved. The first and most vital issue would include understanding the stages of development.

One of the first steps in advocating for your child is allowing yourself time to educate yourself on the elements of the staffing itself. What is the purpose? Who is on the "staffing team"? Reschedule the staffing to allow for your spouse's schedule and/or a provider from another agency with which your child may be receiving services. I would strongly suggest someone go with you, even if both parents are available. Another person can take notes and/or record the staffing.

Talk to your child. Take time to sit down with your child, find out what is bothering him/her. What areas do they *feel* they are struggling at school and why?

Make sure they understand they are not in trouble. This is important from pre-school to grad-school. You want to help them be their best. Look through their homework with them.

Go to the Dept. of Education, request your child's complete school file and DO NOT LEAVE. You do not want anything added or deleted from this file.

In the 1995 Monitoring Report of Iowa's Department of Education demonstrates "(a) in 21 of 58 I.E.P.s, objective criteria were not included, (b) in 14 of 58 I.E.P.s, evaluation schedules were not included." (Office of Special Education Programs Monitoring Report, March 1995, pg. 17)

If and when any evaluations were done, by federal law, you, the parent would have to be notified. Any evaluations would be in the file. Whatever data collected to substantiate the findings of the staffing team would be found in the school files.

An important step to being your own best advocate would be to attempt to locate a child advocate group to assist you. Lawyers and doctors do not represent or treat their own families for good reason. Depending on the severity of your child's and/or where you are in the system, contact your state "Office of Protection and Advocacy." You can find their contact information online. The fact your child is deemed to have a learning disability, behavior disability, with or without a physical impairment makes them eligible for this help. It also means this child is protected under The Individuals with Disabilities Act, The Children With Disabilities Act, I.D.E.A. (IDEA, idea.ed.gov/explore/home 04/17/2016 3:59:54 PM)

Knowledge is power. The parent has the right to have the child evaluated by an outside agency of your choosing.at the expense of the state. You also have the right to request the evaluator be at the staffing, .and, at the very least, implement the supports suggested by the evaluator into the I.E.P.., (Individual Education Program). In fact, input from the parent.is usually imperative to the success of the I.E.P.

Understanding the stages of child development is vital to this process. As parents, we know our children and how exceptional they are. Every child has an area in which they excel. However, they do not all grow and develop at the same rate.

Finally, let me emphasize: Knowledge is Power. This is a fact. Familiarize yourself with The Individuals with Disabilities Education Act, (I.D.E.A). You and your child are protected under this act with very specific language. (idea.ed.gov/explore/home   04/17/2016 3:59:54 P.M.)

UNDERSTANDING STAGES OF DEVELOPMENT

Most theorists will agree on the stages of child development as being eight. We will be looking at the first five. The final three include early to elderly adult.

It is important to remember Erikson and Freud are quite similar in their explanation of the first five stages of early development. However, Erikson attests each stage is identified by a crisis that causes the ego to provide the individual with a balance to delineate between trust and mistrust. In this way he "shifts the emphasis from the id to the reality orientation of the conflict-free ego." He also suggests each crisis moves the individual toward the next stage by successfully resolving the issues. Erikson refers to the ability to manage the crisis as "strengths."

Stage 1 Birth:
Trust verses Mistrust

An infant is dependent on its Mother for food. As the child's needs are met, he develops a trust as well as a self-trust in his ability to cope with stress. This makes the care he receives from his Mother detrimental at this stage. According to Erikson, " it is the quality not the quantity of maternal care that is critical at this stage. Successful resolution will lead to a lasting ego quality of *hope*, an enduring belief wishes can be fulfilled. Unsuccessful resolution will lead to a sense of mistrust in other people and environment." (Robbins, Chatterjee, and Canda: Contemporary Human Behavior Theory, pg. 197.

Stage 2
brings about shame and doubt with ages 2-3.

The child learns "holding on" and "letting go" through the exercise of eliminating bodily waste and holding it to eliminate in the appropriate place. Parents must learn to exercise patience and firmness so the child can learn the correct or accepted manner of control, thus gaining a sense of self-control without losing self-esteem. With this, the child gains an independence and sense of pride. With this the child gains the "lasting ego quality of *will power*, the determination to use free choice and self-restraint. Unsuccessful resolution of this stage will lead to life-long feelings of shame and doubt." (Robbins, Chatterjee, and Canda: pg.197)

Children also gain and refine several more skillful motor skills at this time such as hopping, jumping, and running. "A Three-yr. old. can pedal a tricycle. A Four-yr. old can gallop and a five-yr. old can jump rope and walk on a balance beam. In addition to these gross motor skills – skills that require the use of large muscle groups. Young children develop fine motor skills, including the ability to scribble and draw, cut with scissors and by age 5, print their name. (Hutchinson, 2003, pg. 164)

By age 3, a child is able to successfully complete potty training. By age 4 they are able to, (sometimes very adamantly), dress themselves. There is so much they can do and they want to be independent. The key is having parents who are patient and allow the extra time needed. Spills and messes are imminent; it is how the 'crisis' is resolved which determines the later abilities the child as an adult. Allow spills and messes to happen demonstrating how easy it is to clean it up.

It was not a crisis at all, was it? These little things are immense in the child's self-growth and confidence. The emotional growth of the child can make a world of difference later as an adult. These are all little pieces of the development processes committed to the memory file of the brain.

Some theorists believe the most important stage of cognitive development: the preoperational. Piaget divides this into two sub-stages:

- **Substage 1** is the preconceptual stage which occurs from ages 2-4. Symbolic representation occurs here through the child playing, using symbols and what Piaget referred as deferred imitation. Deferred imitation is exactly what the saw earlier and imitate it. For example, while playing in the early evening, the child pretends to be a cartoon character from his/her favorite morning cartoon show.

- **Sub-stage 2:** the intuitive stage involves ages 4-7, taking us into our next developmental stage. Here objects are represented by language. Earlier ages the child could classify objects identifying two attributes such as size and color. In other words, the child would their stuffed animals by size in the preoperational sub-stage, but in the intuitive su-stage, the child would group them in groups of size and color.

Piaget describes one last preoperational concept as egocentrism. This develops at approximately age 3 where children see themselves as the middle of the universe. This can be problematic for children as they place the blame on themselves for the negatives taking place. For example, 3-yr. old Ron blames himself because his Mother left the family. %=yr. old Ron went to his Grandma's house. Ron smells cookies in the oven and asks her, "Who is having a birthday?"" She answers, "Nobody is having a birthday, they are for the squirrels." Ron keeps waiting for the birthday because that's what happened last time.

- **Language Stage:** Children are asking questions about the world they live in and the environment surrounding them. 3-yr.old's are talking clearly and are usually easy to understand. 4-yr. old's have a remarkable vocabulary and are speaking in 8-10 word sentences. They have a good enough vocabulary to tell a complete story. Most children, at this age, have an understanding of the grammar rules of their culture. According to Hutchinson, they have a clear enough understanding to correct the adults are around them. In addition, they have become little enforcers of the grammar rules due to the fact, they do not have an understanding of the exceptions! ((Hutchinson, 2003, pg. 166)

- **Stage 4** envelops ages 6-12 and is immersed in a whole new environment: the world of public education and the adventures of so many new experiences. In this stage children begin to yearn for recognition and praise from the things they create. This develops competence in the child. Competence is a long lasting and necessary ego quality. Without it follows a lifetime of feeling inadequate and inferior.

- **Stage 5** brings into adolescence at ages 12-18. Puberty takes hold with marked physical and hormonal changes erupting and disrupting any sense of continuity from earlier childhood. Some theorists recognize this stage as the most significant due to the establishing of a "lasting ego identity through signing his or her basic drives, endowments and opportunities. A sense of ego identity is the accrued confidence that one's ability to maintain inner sameness and continuity is matched by the sameness and continuity of one's meaning for others." (Robbins, Chatterjee, and Canda; pg. 198)

It is imperative that as parents, educators and service providers we have a clear and concise understanding of each of these five stages of development and the effect our actions can have. We all want our children to be successful. With that said, we must help them by giving them the best start we possibly can. In order to achieve this goal, we **_must_** see our schools and educators of extensions of our world. We must view them with respect, in a positive light and support them in the classroom to provide a successful academic life for our children.

THE MANY FACES OF INTELLIGENCE

We need to clearly classify intelligence as *smart*. To a great number of the world population this one little word sums up intelligence quite nicely: smart. Oh, how misinformed they are!

I.Q. tests have been identified as measuring linguistics and logical mathematical intelligence. Both are recognized as being culturally biased. This makes it impossible to identify areas of intelligence, skill, and capabilities in which a child excels outside those lines.

Robbins, Chatterjee and Canda list a multitude of cognitive and developmental intelligence types such as:

- "Linguistic Intelligence; a faculty for syntactic and pragmatic language skills, as exemplified by poetry

- Musical Intelligence; the ability to perceive and create pitch (or melody) and rhythm

- Logical Mathematical Intelligence; the prototypical Piagetian intelligence involving ordering and reordering the world of objects and statements in logical ways

- Spatial Intelligence; an "amalgam" of abilities including the ability to accurately perceive the visual world and cognitively manipulate it (as in mentally rotating objects) as well as the ability to find your way in an environment

- Bodily-kinesthetic Intelligence; faculty with fine motor or self-awareness, movement of one's body and skillfully handling objects

- Intrapersonal Intelligence the ability to understand others, to 'notice and make personal distinctions among other individuals and read their moods, temperaments, motivations and intentions.'" (Robbins, Chatterjee and Canda pg. 243)

Emotional Intelligence is another area that encompasses many components of a child's being.

Based on Daniel Goldman's work, emotional intelligence evolves around "five area: knowing one's emotions, or self-awareness; managing emotions, the capacity to soothe one's self and shake off feelings of distress;

motivating one's self, by marshalling emotions in the service of a goal; recognizing emotions in others, or empathy, a fundamental people skill; and handling relationships, the ability to manage others with social competence." (Robbins, Chatterjee, and Canda: pg. 243

When we fail to recognize the emotional aspects of the child, **_we fail the child._**

OBSERVATION LEARNING

The definition of "cognition is the thought processes we used to acquire knowledge." Theorists argue this is the "most distinctive and important" piece of human behavior. We are "conscious, feeling, thinking" creations. As such, we are "constantly seeking out information about our environment." (Psychology Applied to Modern Life: Weiton/Lloyd 1997; pg.50)

Compare a three year old child who has parents and/or siblings who centered around them with a three year old child who is ignored.

Child A is developing through the normal process of talking, singing, walking and playing. Child B who is left in his crib and ignored, appears to have not met the milestones of development. He also appears to be, for lack of a better descriptive, disabled. His growth and development has been retarded simply by the lack of stimulus provided.

The second child has been denied "observational learning." This takes place when a child is responding to or influenced by observing those around them.

Attitudes of the people around the child will also influence the child to a point where they will take on these same attitudes or beliefs without having any understanding of the basis for them. In other words, they will mirror or reflect what they see and hear around them. For years theorists have argued about nurture verses nature. I will not get into it here. I will only point out this important element due to the fact, negative feedback about learning and/or education can have a profound effect on your child.

Observational learning "requires attention, understanding, information and memory." (Weiten/ Lloyd 1997 pg. 50)

"Children learn to be assertive, conscious, self-sufficient, dependable, easy going and so forth by observing others behaving in these ways." (Weiten/Lloyd 1997 pg.50)

A child starting kindergarten knows colors, numbers, the alphabet; depending on the amount of quality time spent with them. This time spent with your child will also cue you as to whether or not your child is having difficulty in any critical areas. The parent should be the first to recognize learning difficulties but that is not always the case. Even the best parent is not a diagnostician.

IDENTIFYING A "LEARNING DISABILITY"

The 1990 Individuals with Disabilities Act provides for "all children the right to a free and appropriate public education and supports the placement of children into integrated settings." (Hutchinson 2003: pg.238)

For a child to feel valued, they need full inclusion. Full inclusion only occurs as a result of integrating their disability along with other aspects of their lives with their family, school and community. This can sometimes create challenges for the parent.

When a child is expected of having a learning disability by a teacher who is licensed and qualified to teach children in this specific age group, the parent must be notified. Before an evaluation can be initiated, by federal law, consent must be obtained from the parent. To prove the problem does not stem from inadequate teaching ability, data must be provided to the parent in the form of written work to substantiate the request. The parent should take this opportunity to ***review the child's complete school records.***

Your child should be observed in the classroom setting. His academic performance and behavior should be documented and observed before he is referred for an evaluation. Just cause must be provided to the parent to substantiate such a request.

"For a child suspected of having a specific learning disability, the documentation of the determination of eligibility, as required in 34 CFR300.306(a)(2), must contain a statement of:

- Whether a child has a specific learning disability; The basis for making the determination, including an assurance that the determination has been made in accordance with 34 CFR 300.306 (©)(1);

- The relevant behavior, if any, noted during the observation of the child and the relationship of that behavior to the child's academic functioning;

- The relevant medical findings, if any;

- Whether the child does not achieve adequately for the child's age or to meet state-approved grade-level standards consistent with 34 CFR 300.309(a)(1), the child does not make sufficient progress to meet age or state-approved grade-level standards consistent with 34 CFR 300.309(a)(2)(i) or the child exhibits a pattern of strengths and weaknesses in performance, achievement, or both, relative to age. state-approved grade-level standards or intellectual development consistent with,34 CFR 300.309(a)(2)(ii);

- The determination of the group concerning the effects of a visual, hearing or motor education services that would be provided; (2) strategies for increasing the child's rate of learning and; (3) ***the parent's right to request an evaluation.***

- The documentation the child's parents were notified about:(1) the State's policies regarding the amount and nature of student performance data that would be collected and the general disability; mental retardation; emotional disturbance; cultural factors; environmental or economic disadvantage; or limited English proficiency on the child's achievement level;

- If a child has participated in a process that assesses the child's response to scientific, research-based intervention: the instructional strategies used and the student-centered data collected; each group must certify in writing whether the report reflects the member's conclusion. If it does not reflect the member's conclusion, the group member must submit a separate statement presenting the member's conclusions. [34 CFR.311] [20 U.S.C. 1221 1401(30);1414(b)(6)]"

(Individuals with Disabilities Education Act (IDEA) Identifying a Learning Disability idea.ed.gov/explore/home 04/17/201603:59:54 P.M.)

THE STAFFING

Each member of the Staffing Team should represent an area addressing the child's needs. Most often there will be the Principal, Teacher from present classroom, Teacher from proposed classroom, Psychiatrist, Social Worker, possibly a separate evaluator, sometimes the Director of the Area Special Education Agency assigned to the school district, and or the Assistant Director. In short, you can expect to be met by at least 4 -5" Specialists." Their specialty of the moment is your child. It can feel quite intimidating, even overwhelming to the parent. It is always a good idea to bring someone with you. Even Uncle Ed, for support.

Upon first notice, ask for a model of your district's staffing procedures so you can familiarize yourself with them.

Hopefully, there is an advocate group near your home, it is worth the money and time to travel to meet them. There is no substitute for knowledge and experience. You will find most often the Advocate you meet has a child in Special Education. The Advocate has acquired the knowledge, training and experience is a direct result of their personal journey. If there is not an advocate available, here are a few tips you may implement, (even with an advocate), bring a reliable note-taker, preferably someone who can actually record the staffing. The point of this is to be able to recall the clearly and concisely relevant talking points. There is a great possibility that you, the parent, will be leaving in a state of shock. You may hear things you never in your wildest dreams thought were part of your child's cognitive, emotional and/or developmental processes. When and if you do not recognize what they are describing about your child, ask questions. Ask for an evaluator(s) of your choice. Instate, out of state it is your child's and your right to request at the expense of the district.

If your child has been receiving services from a provider outside the school system, you may ask them to attend. If they are unable, a written statement with their data, evaluations and suggestions for services and supports. If it is permitted for a Staffing Team member, it is permitted for your provider.

Talk to your parents, siblings, your Pastor, or a close family friend to see if someone can attend the staffing with you. Although it is likely your Advocate will attend, more support never hurts.

The purpose of the staffing is to review findings of the team members who have evaluated and monitored your child's behaviors and needs. If you are not in agreement with the findings, you can request your child be re-evaluated. The ultimate goal is to help your child succeed in school. Try not to view them as the enemy, even if you have had instances where you did not necessarily agree with the teacher.

THE INDIVIDUAL EDUCATION PROGRAM (I.E.P.)

"The public agency must ensure that the IEP Team for each child with a disability includes:

- The parents of the child;

- Not less than one regular education teacher of the child, (If the child is or may be participating in the regular education environment);

- Not less than one special education teacher of the child, or where, not less than one special education provider of the child;

- A member of A representative of the public agency (who has certain specific knowledge and qualifications);

- An individual who can interpret the instructional implications of evaluation results and who also may be one of the other listed members;

- At the discretion of the parent or the agency, other individuals who have knowledge or special expertise regarding the child, relating services, personnel as appropriate; and

- Whenever appropriate, the child whose life is involved.

    ✓ In accordance with 34 CFR 300.321(a)(7), the public agency must invite a child with a disability to attend the child's IEP Team if the purpose of the meeting will be the consideration of the post-secondary goals for the child under the transition services needed to assist the child in reaching those goals under 34 CFR 300.320(b). [34 CFR 300.321(a) and (b)(1)] [20 U.S.C. 1414(d)(1)(B)]

    ✓ A member of the IEP Team described in 34 CFR300.321(a)(2) through (a)(5) is not required to attend an IEP meeting, in whole or in part, if the parent of the child and the public agency agree, in writing, that the attendance of the member is not necessary because the member's area of the curriculum or related services is not being discussed in the meeting

✓ A member of the IEP Team described in 34 CFR 300.321(a)(2) through (a)(5) may be excused from attending an IEP Meeting, in whole or in part, when the meeting involves a modification to or a discussion of the member's area of the curriculum or related services, if:

> ➤ The parent, in writing and the public agency consent to the excusal;

> ➤ The member submits, in writing to the parent and the IEP Team with input the development of the IEP prior to the meeting.

[34 CFR 300.321(e) [20 U>S.C. 1414(d)(1)(©)

Provide for inviting representatives from the part C system.

- The notice required under 34 CFR 300.322(a)(1) (regarding an IEP meeting), among other things, must inform the parents of the provisions in 34 CFR300.321(a)(6) and (c) (relating to the participation of other individuals on the IEP Team who have knowledge or special expertise about the child), and 34 CFR In the case of a child with a disability aged three thrrrrrrrrrrrrrrrr300.321(f) (relating to the participation of the Part C service coordinator or other representatives of the Part C system at the initial IEP Team meeting for a child previously served under Part C of the IDEA).

[34 CFR .300.322(b)(1)]" (idea.ed.gov/explore/home 04/17/201603:59:54 P.M.)

- "Set forth provisions regarding considerations of individualized Family Service Plans, (IFSPs), for children aged three through five.

  - ✓ In the case of a child with a disability aged three through five, (or, at the discretion of the state educational agency, (SEA), a two-year-old child with a disability who will turn three during the school year), the IEP Team must consider an IFSP that contains the IFSP content, (including the natural environments statement), described in section 636(d) of the IDEA and its implementing regulations, (including an educational component that promotes school readiness and incorporates pre-literacy, language, and numeracy skills for children with IFSPs under 34 CFR 300.323 who are at least 3 years of age), and that is developed in accordance with the IEP procedures under Part B. The ISFP may serve as the IEP is consistent with state policy and agreed to by the agency and the child's parents.

✓ In implementing these ISFP provisions, the public agency must provide to the child's parents, a detailed explanation of the difference between an ISFP and an IEP. If the parents choose an ISFP, the public agency must obtain written informed consent from the parents.

[34 CFR 300.323(b)] [20 U.S.C. 1414(d)(2)(B)]

- Require the IEP be accessible to teachers and others responsible for its implementation. Each public agency must ensure:

  ✓ The child's IEP is accessible to each regular education teacher, special education teacher, related services provider who is responsible for its implementation.

  ✓ Each teacher and provider described in this provision, is informed of his or her specific responsibilities related to implementing the child's IEP and the specific accommodations, modifications, and supports that must be provided for the child in accordance with the IEP.

[34 CFR 300.323(d)]" (idea.ed.gov/explore/home 04/17/ 201603:59:54 P.M)"

This is your child. Your input is valuable. You know what your child responds to best. The IEP should reflect this. Do **_not_** let the Team dictate the terms involved here. "Specific accommodations" can include anything from assistance with comprehension to oral testing, even extra bathroom breaks.

By the time of the scheduled staffing, hopefully you have had time to review the findings of any and all evaluations, as well as time to consult with your own providers.

Knowledge is power. This is the part of the staffing where the parent has the power to ensure this plan is best. It can accommodate the needs of the child. It is also the time to review past plans to determine whether or not they have been implemented, to what degree and was there improvement. If you have had the opportunity to review your child's complete school file, you will be familiar with these factors.

Knowledge is Power

Knowledge is power. The more prepared you are for the school staffing, the more valuable you will be as a member of the staffing team. You are a vital member of the staffing because no-one knows more about your child than you. You are the expert. Be informed and well-prepared to do justice for your child.

REFERENCES

American Heritage Dictionary, pg. 13, 1994.

Amrican Flag, (Cover Picture)4:45 p.m. 04/14/2021

https://www.publicdomainpictures.net/
pictures/90000/velka/american-flag-hear

Dimensions of Human Behavior, The Changing
Life Course, Second Edition, pg. .237; Elizabeth D.
Hutchinson pg.164,168, 238

I.D.E.A. (IDEA, idea.ed.gov/explore/home 04/17/2016
3:59:54 PM)

Individuals with Disabilities Education Act (IDEA)
Identifying a Learning Disability idea.ed.gov/explore/
home 04/17/201603:59:54 P.M

Office of Protection and Advocacy

Office of Special Education Programs Monitoring Report, March 1995, pg. 17

Robbins, Chatterjee, and Canda: pg.197, 198, 238, 243

Weiten/Lloyd 1997 pg. 50